The Easter Story
ACCORDING TO MATTHEW

And it came to pass, when Jesus had finished all these sayings, He said unto His disciples, Ye know that after two days is the feast of the Passover, and the Son of man is betrayed to be crucified.

Matthew 26:1–2

The story of our Savior's

death and resurrection

is presented to

....

....

by

....

....

The Easter Story

ACCORDING TO MATTHEW

Illustrated by DONALD KUEKER
for Concordia Publishing House
with text from the King James Version of the Bible

CONCORDIA PUBLISHING HOUSE • SAINT LOUIS

Then assembled together the chief priests, and the scribes, and the elders of the people, unto the palace of the high priest, who was called Caiaphas, and consulted that they might take Jesus by subtlety, and kill Him.

Matthew 26:3–4

One of the twelve, called Judas Iscariot, went unto the chief priests, and said unto them, What will ye give me, and I will deliver Him unto you? And they covenanted with him for thirty pieces of silver. And from that time he sought opportunity to betray Him.

Matthew 26:14–16

Now when the even was come, [Jesus] sat down with the twelve. And as they did eat, He said, Verily I say unto you, that one of you shall betray Me.

And they were exceeding sorrowful, and began every one of them to say unto Him, Lord, is it I?

And He answered and said, He that dippeth His hand with Me in the dish, the same shall betray Me.

The Son of Man goeth as it is written of Him: but woe unto that man by whom the Son of Man is betrayed! It had been good for that man if he had not been born.

Then Judas, which betrayed Him, answered and said, Master, is it I? He said unto him, Thou hast said.

Matthew 26:20–25

And as they were eating, Jesus took bread, and blessed it, and brake it, and gave it to the disciples, and said, Take, eat; this is My body.

And He took the cup, and gave thanks, and gave it to them, saying, Drink ye all of it; for this is My blood of the new testament, which is shed for many for the remission of sins.

Matthew 26:26–28

Then cometh Jesus with them unto a place called Gethsemane, and saith unto the disciples, Sit ye here, while I go and pray yonder. And He took with Him Peter and the two sons of Zebedee, and began to be sorrowful and very heavy.

Then saith He unto them, My soul is exceeding sorrowful, even unto death: tarry ye here, and watch with Me.

And He went a little farther, and fell on His face, and prayed, saying, O My Father, if it be possible, let this cup pass from Me: nevertheless not as I will, but as thou wilt.

… Then cometh He to His disciples, and saith unto them, Sleep on now, and take your rest: behold, the hour is at hand, and the Son of man is betrayed into the hands of sinners. Rise, let us be going: behold, he is at hand that doth betray Me.

Matthew 26:36–46

And while He yet spake, lo, Judas, one of the twelve, came, and with him a great multitude with swords and staves, from the chief priests and elders of the people. Now he that betrayed Him gave them a sign, saying, Whomsoever I shall kiss, that same is He: hold Him fast. And forthwith he came to Jesus, and said, Hail, Master; and kissed Him.

And Jesus said unto him, Friend, wherefore art thou come? Then came they, and laid hands on Jesus and took Him. …

But all this was done, that the scriptures of the prophets might be fulfilled. Then all the disciples forsook him, and fled.

Matthew 26:47–56

And they that had laid hold on Jesus led Him away to Caiaphas the high priest, where the scribes and the elders were assembled. …

Now the chief priests, and elders, and all the council, sought false witness against Jesus, to put Him to death; but found none: yea, though many false witnesses came, yet found they none. At the last came two false witnesses, and said, This fellow said, I am able to destroy the temple of God, and to build it in three days.

And the high priest arose, and said unto Him, Answerest Thou nothing? What is it which these witness against Thee?

But Jesus held His peace, And the high priest answered and said unto Him, I adjure Thee by the living God, that Thou tell us whether Thou be the Christ, the Son of God.

Jesus saith unto him, Thou hast said: nevertheless I say unto you, Hereafter shall ye see the Son of man sitting on the right hand of power, and coming in the clouds of heaven.

Then the high priest rent his clothes, saying, He hath spoken blasphemy; what further need have we of witnesses? Behold, now ye have heard His blasphemy. What think ye? They answered and said, He is guilty of death.

Matthew 26:57–66

When the morning was come, all the chief priests and elders of the people took counsel against Jesus to put Him to death: And when they had bound Him, they led Him away, and delivered Him to Pontius Pilate the governor.

Then Judas, which had betrayed Him, when he saw that He was condemned, repented himself, and brought again the thirty pieces of silver to the chief priests and elders, saying, I have sinned in that I have betrayed the innocent blood. And they said, What is that to us? see thou to that.

And he cast down the pieces of silver in the temple, and departed, and went and hanged himself. And the chief priests took the silver pieces, and … bought with them the potter's field, to bury strangers in. Wherefore that field was called, The field of blood, unto this day.

Matthew 27:1–8

Now at that feast the governor was wont to release unto the people a prisoner, whom they would. And they had then a notable prisoner, called Barabbas. Therefore when they were gathered together, Pilate said unto them, Whom will ye that I release unto you? Barabbas, or Jesus which is called Christ? For he knew that for envy they had delivered Him. … But the chief priests and elders persuaded the multitude that they should ask Barabbas, and destroy Jesus.

… Pilate saith unto them, What shall I do then with Jesus which is called Christ? They all say unto him, Let Him be crucified. And the governor said, Why, what evil hath He done? But they cried out the more, saying, Let Him be crucified.

When Pilate saw that he could prevail nothing, but that rather a tumult was made, he took water, and washed his hands before the multitude, saying, I am innocent of the blood of this just person: see ye to it. Then answered all the people, and said, His blood be on us, and on our children.

Then released he Barabbas unto them: and when he had scourged Jesus, he delivered Him to be crucified.

Matthew 27:15–26

Then the soldiers of the governor took Jesus into the common hall, and gathered unto Him the whole band of soldiers. And they stripped Him, and put on Him a scarlet robe.

And when they had platted a crown of thorns, they put it upon His head, and a reed in His right hand: and they bowed the knee before Him, and mocked Him, saying, Hail, King of the Jews! And they spit upon Him, and took the reed, and smote Him on the head.

And after that they had mocked Him, they took the robe off from Him, and put His own raiment on Him, and led Him away to crucify Him.

Matthew 27:27–31

And when they were come unto a place called Golgotha, that is to say, a place of a skull, they gave Him vinegar to drink mingled with gall: and when He had tasted thereof, He would not drink.

And they crucified Him. ... And sitting down they watched Him there; and set up over His head His accusation written, THIS IS JESUS THE KING OF THE JEWS.

Then were there two thieves crucified with Him, one on the right hand, and another on the left. And they that passed by reviled Him, wagging their heads, and saying, Thou that destroyest the temple, and buildest it in three days, save Thyself. If Thou be the Son of God, come down from the cross.

Likewise also the chief priests mocking Him, with the scribes and elders, said, He saved others; Himself He cannot save. If He be the King of Israel, let Him now come down from the cross, and we will believe Him. He trusted in God; let Him deliver Him now, if He will have Him: for He said, I am the Son of God.

Matthew 27:33–43

Now from the sixth hour there was darkness over all the land unto the ninth hour. And about the ninth hour Jesus cried with a loud voice, saying, Eli, Eli, lama sabachthani? That is to say, My God, My God, why hast Thou forsaken Me?

Some of them that stood there, when they heard that, said, This man calleth for Elias. And straightway one of them ran, and took a sponge, and filled it with vinegar, and put it on a reed, and gave Him to drink. The rest said, Let be, let us see whether Elias will come to save Him.

Jesus, when He had cried again with a loud voice, yielded up the ghost.

And, behold, the veil of the temple was rent in twain from the top to the bottom; and the earth did quake, and the rocks rent. …

Now when the centurion, and they that were with him, watching Jesus, saw the earthquake, and those things that were done, they feared greatly, saying, Truly this was the Son of God.

Matthew 27:45–54

When the even was come, there came a rich man of Arimathaea, named Joseph, who also himself was Jesus' disciple: He went to Pilate, and begged the body of Jesus. Then Pilate commanded the body to be delivered.

And when Joseph had taken the body, he wrapped it in a clean linen cloth, and laid it in his own new tomb, which he had hewn out in the rock: and he rolled a great stone to the door of the sepulchre, and departed.

And there was Mary Magdalene, and the other Mary, sitting over against the sepulchre.

Matthew 27:57–61

Now the next day, that followed the day of the preparation, the chief priests and Pharisees came together unto Pilate, saying, Sir, we remember that that deceiver said, while He was yet alive, After three days I will rise again. Command therefore that the sepulchre be made sure until the third day, lest His disciples come by night, and steal Him away, and say unto the people, He is risen from the dead: so the last error shall be worse than the first.

Pilate said unto them, Ye have a watch: go your way, make it as sure as ye can.

So they went, and made the sepulchre sure, sealing the stone, and setting a watch.

Matthew 27:62–66

In the end of the sabbath, as it began to dawn toward the first day of the week, came Mary Magdalene and the other Mary to see the sepulchre. And, behold, there was a great earthquake: for the angel of the Lord descended from heaven, and came and rolled back the stone from the door, and sat upon it. His countenance was like lightning, and his raiment white as snow: And for fear of him the keepers did shake, and became as dead men.

And the angel answered and said unto the women, Fear not ye: for I know that ye seek Jesus, which was crucified. He is not here: for He is risen, as He said. Come, see the place where the Lord lay. And go quickly, and tell His disciples that He is risen from the dead; and, behold, He goeth before you into Galilee; there shall ye see Him: lo, I have told you.

And they departed quickly from the sepulchre with fear and great joy; and did run to bring His disciples word.

Matthew 28:1–8

And as they went to tell His disciples, behold, Jesus met them, saying, All hail. And they came and held Him by the feet, and worshipped Him. Then said Jesus unto them, Be not afraid: go tell My brethren that they go into Galilee, and there shall they see Me.

Now when they were going, behold, some of the watch came into the city, and shewed unto the chief priests all the things that were done. And when they were assembled with the elders, and had taken counsel, they gave large money unto the soldiers, saying, Say ye, His disciples came by night, and stole Him away while we slept. And if this come to the governor's ears, we will persuade him, and secure you. So they took the money, and did as they were taught: and this saying is commonly reported among the Jews until this day.

Matthew 28:9–15

Then the eleven disciples went away into Galilee, into a mountain where Jesus had appointed them. And when they saw Him, they worshipped Him: but some doubted.

And Jesus came and spake unto them, saying, All power is given unto Me in heaven and in earth. Go ye therefore, and teach all nations, baptizing them in the name of the Father, and of the Son, and of the Holy Ghost: Teaching them to observe all things whatsoever I have commanded you: and, lo, I am with you always, even unto the end of the world. Amen.

Matthew 28:16–20